STEERING LINKEDIN FOR OPTIMUM SALES AND LEAD GENERATION

THE COMPLETE GUIDE TO SOCIAL SELLING EXPERTISE ON LINKEDIN MARKET

By
EMILE MARTIN

TABLE OF CONTENTS

INTRODUCTION

"My time is too limited to use LinkedIn"
"I find technology to move too quickly!"
"I fear that I will make a mistake."
"How can I accomplish this?"
The key to LinkedIn marketing is this: with a very modest time and financial effort, you can generate a lot of leads, establish credibility with your target demographic, and establish an excellent reputation.

Marketing on LinkedIn is not a magic bullet. It is up to you to use it to your advantage. This implies that you cannot use LinkedIn without first deciding why you want to use it and what you want to achieve in the short- and long-term. It almost takes no effort to complete.

To do it correctly and get the greatest results, you'll need knowledge, time, dedication, and maybe a little money. The sad remains of haphazard efforts at participation and half-baked accounts abound on LinkedIn, leading many users to declare, "LinkedIn just doesn't work for me!" The instrument is not defective. It's the methodology. It's simple to set up your profile. Developing a plan for involvement is not.

Would you want to:
> Increase your responsiveness to customers.
> Raise awareness of a product or service?
> Take consumer opinion into account while developing new products.
> Become more proficient in branding?
> Boost your visibility online?
> Become an authority in the field?

All of these are excellent reasons for using LinkedIn.
"The majority of company owners can maintain a highly acceptable social media presence in six hours a week, including research and production work, according to the latest 2010 Social Media Marketing Industry Report."

Fantastic! Let's now discover how to accomplish it even more quickly, produce greater outcomes, and get over typical obstacles to successful social media marketing.

CHAPTER 1: THE GOLD MINE LINKEDIN MARKETING

Registered users of LinkedIn may have a contact list of reputable and well-known business people. A member can "connect" with other members of the same group or to welcome visitors to the site.

The connections list may be helpful in:

- ❖ constructing a three-degree-deep trustworthy network. (First, second, and third-degree links)
- ❖ Meeting people via member introductions who you would find difficult to connect with in another way
- ❖ Looking for a job or a candidate?
- ❖ Finding Business Possibilities
- ❖ Getting Suggestions from Other People
- ❖ Pursuing relationships
- ❖ Keeping up with the businesses where your contacts work

Bringing your offer to the attention of certain prospects Professionals must already be familiar with one another or have a pre-existing connection to use LinkedIn's "gated-access approach." This technique differs significantly from Facebook's.

In May 2003, Reid Hoffman and many key figures from socialnet.com and Paypal founded LinkedIn. With locations in Omaha, Chicago, New York, and London, the company's main office is located in Mountain View, California. Former Yahoo! Inc. executive Jeff Weiner is the CEO of LinkedIn at the moment. The current chairman of the board is Reid Hoffman.

As of right now, LinkedIn claims to have 100 million users, with one new member joining every second. The United States makes up about 50% of the membership. Of these, almost 11 million are European. The nation with the quickest growth is India. China is also joining the fray. As of the time of writing, LinkedIn was valued at over $2 billion, according to Bloomberg.

No matter how much time or money you invest, an egg beater cannot be used to construct a home. To make sure your efforts are not in vain, make sure you have selected the appropriate network for your company strategy. Facebook's B2C (business-to-consumer) strategy is the most effective for some businesses. For professional service providers in the B2B (business-to-business) market, LinkedIn is the ideal option.

The emergence of new technology is gradually altering this reality. Ray Brown, the creator of Clienteerhub, used the term "B2Me" recently to describe a cross-functional, two-way area where customer input is paramount.

 Ray told me lately that it's not about making money right away. It goes beyond simple

marketing to include the whole company idea.
"The beginning point for utilizing LinkedIn (or,
for that matter, any social networking platform)
is to ask yourself, "Is this technology suitable for
my business?" according to HubSpot's guide,
How to Generate Leads utilizing LinkedIn. It
isn't always a good idea to follow the path only
because others have followed it, after all.

CHAPTER 2: ACHIEVING SUCCESS ON LINKEDIN IN FIVE EASY STEPS

Social media marketing provides you with the most effective means of communicating your narrative when it comes to marketing. Businesses like Starbucks on Facebook, Zappos on Twitter, Graco on Flickr, The Personal Branding Network on LinkedIn, and Dell everywhere that have successfully created vibrant online communities have discovered:

I. Who they are (as seen by the people)
II. How to draw in customers
III. Reasons for investors to support the company's narrative

What is your business's history? What are your beliefs? What qualities do you want people to identify with you, your audience? I created The Confident Copywriter brand because I was fed up with the copywriting industry's then-common "make-six-figures-by-next-Tuesday" hype (2006). I believed I had found a vulnerability and that my "genuine" point of view would be well-received by the "average" copywriter. It seems that I was correct. The Confident Copywriter was well received and served as a springboard for my discussion on other subjects today. You undoubtedly have a tale to share. Let's discuss how to express it.

A. PLANNING: MEDIA ACTION PLAN FOR ONLINE AND STRATEGY

How should your LinkedIn marketing campaign be planned in the first place? By comprehending the rationale behind your first selection of LinkedIn. "Because everyone else is doing it" is insufficient justification.

If anything, LinkedIn is the best tool for generating leads. And a company cannot thrive without high-quality leads. According to a recent analysis by Marketing Sherpa, a survey revealed that B2B marketers are more concerned with producing quality leads than with driving fresh demand for their goods and services.

Maybe marketers in 2010 are simply more aware of the problem with demand generation within their companies and know that effective sales depend on having high-quality leads.
According to trends, most B2B companies are spending more on inbound marketing strategies to provide their sales teams with more leads of a higher quality.
In general, the following objectives should be the focus of your LinkedIn program:

1.Creating a buzz around a product, service, or brand

2. An increase in public brand awareness overall

3. More visitors to strengthen SEO initiatives

4. More blog followers to foster a more vibrant community

5. More and higher quality leads

6. Merely tracking public perceptions and comments about a brand

7. Higher income and sales
Assume that one morning when Joe the Businessman wakes up, he thinks to himself, "My company is way behind." We are being killed by our competitors! We urgently need additional clients. I really need to go on that social networking thing that everyone is talking about.

He so creates a rudimentary LinkedIn profile, joins a few groups, and then logs out. and holds out. He gets in touch with me soon after, lamenting that while he "did what he was supposed to," social media "just doesn't work for me." (Also, this is a true story). Name altered to keep the ignorant safe.)

In a sense, Joe has failed. He didn't carry out his assigned tasks. He didn't put in much effort, had no goal, no strategy, wasn't engaged, and didn't know how to use LinkedIn properly. Hell, it would be a miracle if Joe were to succeed! The lesson here is that you need to have a plan. Sure, it's not an enjoyable element, but it's an essential one.

B. INDUSTRY BRANDING VS. NICHE BRANDING

Every business owner, even those with highly specialized interests, can now locate a core audience, grow their firm, and achieve success thanks to the Internet. A tiny group of individuals who are drawn to the author's distinct point of view have created a plethora of forums, blogs, and websites. This is fantastic since it shows how anybody with only a topic interest can launch an internet company.

People are serious when they claim that the Internet has levelled the playing field! To be considered "successful" in your specialty, you no longer need to compete with retailers like Target or Walmart.
Let's assume, more broadly, that you practice personal injury law or are a certified public accountant. How can one effectively carve out a place for themselves in an industry this size?

Starting with a more narrowly defined market is the best course of action. Creating resources for that more narrowly defined target market enhances the value of your offerings. Expert status may be developed via e-books, reports, public speaking, free or paid seminars, and community service geared toward small groups' interests.

 From this vantage point, it is simple to see how your LinkedIn marketing efforts may be made more efficient at the planning stage, which will help you become more successful in your market by making the process of creating, implementing, and promoting a quicker road to success more efficient. This does not mean that you have to remain there indefinitely. Innovation, development, and change are essential to your company's future. Focus on the areas where you can be most effective and influential if you want to sell yourself on LinkedIn. For instance, I have training and education in copywriting, conversion rate optimization (CRO), and search engine optimization (SEO). I still write a lot of material for my clients, but SEO is just too complicated for this right-brained person like me. I would rather position myself more widely as an expert in Internet marketing with skills in a number of important domains, such as SEO and CRO.

You've undoubtedly heard of cleaning services that only clean commercial buildings, realtors who exclusively list luxury homes for sale, gourmet food stores that exclusively offer gourmet foods, and copywriters who specialize in whitepapers.

By concentrating on their areas of expertise and true passions, these businesses are able to draw in audiences and discover their own special strength. If you are putting a lot of effort into your LinkedIn marketing but are not seeing results, you could be attempting to "fit a square peg into a round hole," which means you are losing out on important opportunities to connect with like-minded individuals, hanging out in the wrong groups, or missing out on your primary areas of interest. That shouldn't be too difficult! If so, something isn't quite right. These pointers will help you get going:

1.Seek assistance for profile optimization. Even for as little as $50, I can assist you.

2. Edit your synopsis. Don't just copy and paste your CV. Show off your individuality!

3. Fill up your profile completely.

4. Take another photo if needed. grin broadly,
gazing directly at the audience. Don't you want
to do more business?

5. Above all, take a break from your profile and
start interacting! Join groups on LinkedIn,
contribute your knowledge, and volunteer to
help others achieve. Here's where real
interaction and lead creation start.

C. IMPLEMENTATION: BUILDING AND PLANNING OF PROFILE

I've seen entrepreneurs say things like, "We
really don't have a specific market." What? Let's
consider this for a little while.
We'll use dirt as an illustration.

One may argue that because everyone needs soil,
there is no particular market for the "dirt seller."
I beg to disagree, however. More soil is needed
by gardening enthusiasts than by cyclists. Dirt is

more necessary to landscape firms than opera singers. More soil is needed by construction businesses than by owners of retail stores.

There is a target market for each product. It's your task to locate it! The client is the main priority these days. You will be one step closer to success when you can ascertain what your audience really wants as opposed to what you believe they want.

Another excellent example is McDonald's. Surely everyone must eat? However, McDonald's patrons want a certain value: quickness, cost-effectiveness, and ease things you would not get at a regular sit-down restaurant. McDonald's has introduced "healthier" options as customers' concerns about avoiding its high-fat, high-calorie, high-sodium, and low-fibre menu items have grown. But let's face it, the business has never been and will never be recognized for its salads. But I dare you to go to any McDonald's in the country and discover a cheeseburger that tastes "different."

It is not going to occur.

How do they accomplish that? The company is aware of what a McDonald's cheeseburger is and what each and every consumer, regardless of location, expects. McDonald's does not mislead its customers. Rather, the company honors the client by sticking to a formula week after week, even while there are sporadic excursions into salad territory.
How can you meet the needs of your purchasing audience?

1. Engage in interaction, but do it in a proper manner.
2. Above and above expectations
3. Honour your word.
4. Honour the client, but first and foremost, get to know them. All set to go to the exciting next phase: marriage? It's nearly here.

Point to Keep in Mind: The success of your LinkedIn profile depends on accurately identifying and targeting your audience, as well as on meeting them where they are, sharing, and offering relevant information at the appropriate moment.

D. APPLICATIONS WITHOUT HABITATION

Hence, preparation is necessary for implementation, which is described as "the realization of an application, or execution of a plan, idea, model, design, specification. standard, algorithm, or policy."
Select the appropriate social media platform for the image of your brand. Creating and sustaining an "everywhere" presence will also dilute it, resulting in expenses and effort spent, as well as increased irritation.

Think carefully about who will carry out your LinkedIn marketing strategy.

As the quality of your campaign is the key to its success, seek assistance as required.

It's normal to see a doctor when you're unwell, to have your loud automobile serviced, and to call a reliable roofer when your roof leaks, so don't be frightened to contact an expert. Keep in mind that saving money is not your main objective when it comes to your LinkedIn success. Your objective is to get
outcomes.

Content is king! While LinkedIn is a fantastic resource, remember that people read and make judgments about what to buy. Engage them with relevant and engaging information.

Consider your target audience's requirements. This necessitates understanding your audience, including how to contact them, where to locate them, and what they
desire.

Recall that you are under observation. be
thrilling to hear your name brought up in relation
to a trending issue; but, enormous power also
with great responsibility.

You have to market yourself more cautiously the
greater the following you have.

Not all customers are on the lookout for freebies.
Once again, understanding your target will help
you develop the services and offerings that will
forge a solid following and establish you as their
authority.

E. CONVERSATIONS FOR STARTERS

Take into account the requirements of both your
followers on LinkedIn and your
firm's immediate and long-term objectives. Here
are some topics for discussion:

Information about a company or brand provides
value and reveals "personality."

The only task fun information asks of its readers
is to enjoy themselves!

News releases
Creating events: online, offline, or mixed
Requesting and answering feedback
Coverage of global events or industry news
Personal acknowledgment (birthdays,
promotions, accomplishments, etc.) Customer
service counts
Polls, quizzes, and surveys
Adding a thought-provoking quotation to
another "just for fun" item: new software
innovations that improve our quality of life
Recall: Maintain attention to purposeful,
pertinent, and helpful message
Be present; that is, avoid being robotic. Allow
your individuality to come through!

Be sincere.
When someone responds in the moment to
anything significant you've done or said, you
have your followers. The days of the

self-serving, self-promotional brand message are long gone. Companies listen to what customers have to say these days as they understand that customers have a plethora of options and may quickly switch brands.

Make sure the participants in your LinkedIn initiatives have an enjoyable and stimulating experience. Upon launching my LinkedIn group, Social Media for the Clueless, I received several messages, both publicly and privately, criticizing me for using the phrase "clueless" and accusing me of "demeaning people," "alienating potential members," and other foolishness. Naturally, the group name was a satirical allusion, taken from my first ebook's title, but not everyone understood it.

All I knew was that the name spoke to me, and I thought others would feel the same way. (Such criticism might hurt, but it can also offer a highly effective platform for debate). We got over 500 members in a matter of days, and we now had 63 talks in progress! And we haven't stopped yet. I use this example to show how challenging conventional wisdom may be, having a little fun, and presenting an alternative (not insulting or harsh)

A point of view may agitate the situation just enough to elicit a favorable response. Indeed, having fun on LinkedIn is OK, but not to the extent that it calls for donning a lampshade (check out Facebook for that type of fun!).

F. WHO MANAGES THE SHIP?

A captain is necessary for every LinkedIn marketing campaign. When you operate alone, you're that. When working in a group setting, coworkers might provide suggestions,
But one person can only control the ship. Marketing on LinkedIn takes patience. It cannot be avoided. Meanwhile, your business is working toward a lot of other goals, such as profitability.

According to digital branding specialist Brian
Solis in The Ten Stages of Social Media
Business Integration: "The transition from
instinctive reaction to deliberate, strategic
Both parties will benefit from communication.
We are able to create really engaging messaging
and content at this point. We have to offer the
audience something to believe in, something that
moves them, in order to keep it going.
Our shared talks create a human algorithm that
acts as the brand-worthy persona is established
via implementation, which is closely related to
the "pulse of awareness, trustworthiness, and
emotion." In addition to having a goal (the
strategy), your LinkedIn activity has to influence
customers and mold the brand message
(implementation).

 Maybe you've heard of the "brand makeover,"
when a company's website or landing page
becomes utterly outdated as it builds a more
active community.

The brand makeover ensures a considerably more enjoyable customer experience by redefining the company's purpose, which is customer engagement.

CHAPTER 3: LINKEDIN MARKETING MANAGER

If there are two or more persons working for your organization, assign blame.
for changes to the material. creating and updating relevant material on a regular basis Even with the correct technologies, managing material for a variety of audiences, maintaining social significance, and answering inquiries and comments are all demanding tasks.

These responsibilities may be handled by the marketing or communications departments of bigger businesses. Unless you decide to contract out all or part of your LinkedIn marketing to an expert, you are responsible for everything when you work alone.

In any case, a crucial step in the implementation process is communication. In summary, if you

are unable to manage, get assistance. Barter:
Spend as much as necessary to complete the
task.
Don't give the work to the first person who
comes in the room, even if you believe your staff
members could accomplish it.
Your LinkedIn marketing manager becomes the
public face and voice of
your company. It's a crucial position.

A. "WHY CAN'T I JUST CREATE A PROFILE AND GO INDIRECTLY?"

Simply put, no.
The key to LinkedIn marketing that works best
is sharing experiences, important relationships
and insightful data, gradually establishing a
company's presence through community
development, attentive listening, and sincere
involvement. Because social media is always
evolving, these phases signify a certain point in
time. They'll keep developing and growing.
using novel experiences and technology.

Social media is ultimately a luxury and a tool, providing you with one more chance to manage a more significant and relevant company. (Brian Solis)

LinkedIn marketing involves far more than just creating a profile and wishing for success. One is anticipatory, whereas the other is not.
The CEO of The Network, Luis Ramos, states that developing a successful LinkedIn marketing strategy is difficult since "it involves looking outside the organization to determine the proper degree of engagement, as well as looking inside the organization to establish appropriate practices, usage policies, and content parameters."

CHAPTER 4: COOPERATION FOR OPTIMUM PRODUCTIVITY

LinkedIn first and foremost demands that users connect and only by invitation. One extends an invitation; the other responds. A non-member you invite must join in order for them to accept your invitation.

A "first-degree" link is formed when someone accepts your direct invitation. LinkedIn highly advises that you carefully consider who you will Invite only those you know and trust, such as friends, relatives, coworkers, or classmates from the past or present. We go into further detail in this book on the need of expanding your presence by venturing outside of this close-knit neighborhood. what you decide upon while making a choice.

LI anticipates that you will eventually ask a first-degree connection for a recommendation or the other way around. For this reason, quantity is not nearly as crucial as quality. Granted, boasting about having hundreds of connections is entertaining. Members of the LinkedIn network are chosen rather than gathered, in contrast to Facebook.

In the LinkedIn network, recommendations may also raise page rank. Improved relationships and improved lead production might be associated with a higher rank. A higher rank describes your position on a list that appears when a member does a keyword search. Similar to Google, the majority of users just browse the first page of results while looking for what they're looking for. This implies that you must attend.

LinkedIn said in 2008 that making connections with anyone and everyone may be "counterproductive." This misconception still exists today. Many users' profiles are neglected since they are unsure about whether or not to interact.

It's true that people you know and trust should make up the majority of your LI network, but it would be silly to deliberately avoid interacting with anybody else. "It pains me to see when people only have fewer than 100 connections and they think that having a "small trusted network" is the way to go," says LinkedIn author Lewis Howes. That's a joke, and those who think that way will be wondering why their message isn't reaching more people and why they haven't met their marketing objectives.

You never know where an opportunity or significant advancement may come from. You will only be exposed to a restricted number of possibilities inside a small network if you simply exchange ideas with individuals you already know and don't reach out to make new connections.

When it comes to connecting, marketing whiz Chris Brogan says, Here's where LinkedIn wishes I would stop talking. I see connections differently than others do. Anybody may communicate with me. There doesn't seem to be much of a drawback to using the service to connect. I believe that via interacting with others, I'm creating possible networks that will allow others to find and get in touch with other like-minded individuals.

Although I have some extremely well-known contacts who may not share my views, I do sometimes decline requests for connection forwarding. Overall, however, I think it's perfectly acceptable to make the offer. Without a doubt, quality comes first. I'm not in favour of connecting for the purpose of smug entitlements. It's absurd to say, "My network is bigger than yours." It makes sense if we use the six degrees of separation theory, which is the basis for LinkedIn's creation:

The concept of "six degrees of separation," also known as the "Human Web," states that each person on Earth is, on average, six steps away from another person. As a result, a chain of "a friend of a friend" statements can be made to connect any two people in six steps or less. The Wall Street Journal recommends the following topics for businesses using LinkedIn marketing for the first time:

How LinkedIn will fit into the main business plan

Who will be the company's "voice"?

How much time is going to be spent on LinkedIn tasks?

How soon the business will assess its performance

When it comes time to put out flames, who else will be on the team?

B. LISTENING: LINKEDIN MARKETING'S POWER

Listening is the most crucial social media activity. LinkedIn marketing, in contrast to conventional marketing, requires you to provide your audience with the tools, goods, and services that they most want. You have to listen to find out what it is.

As an example, I dealt with a customer lately who looked confused even after asking me a lot of questions on the terms of engagement.
As it happened, a few days later, she proudly gave me her first "discussion": more like a sales pitch or a call to action: "Learn
learn more about this fantastic possibility for a home business!"

It goes without saying that the group administrator promptly relocated the post to the appropriate section, Promotions. My customer just didn't understand. A lesson on opening her ears was in order as well as going back to the drafting board.

Lisa Barone, Outspoken Media's Chief Branding Officer and co-founder, said, "Your role is to assist, listen, and spread the word only when suitable. Every ten to fifteen communications in which you assist someone else, you chance to add a self-promotional one. That is all.

 This isn't [LinkedIn] about you. It's all about getting to know your clients and making a connection with them so that they will remember you as their buddy who specializes in X when they need it.

Engagement undoubtedly requires excellent (read: meaningful, relevant) dialogue. However, talks conducted online lack the customary communicative cues such as expressions on the face or body. What more might you do to make sure your message is understood correctly?

C. 21 LINKEDIN ENGAGEMENT TIPS

Emile Martin compiled the following list:
1. Find all relevant communities of interest and pay attention to the decisions, difficulties, perceptions, and desires of the members of each network.
2. Don't simply engage in your own domains. Engage where it is beneficial and required for you to be there.
3. Establish the personality, identity, and character of the brand and
compare it to the internet personas of those who represent it.
4. Name a point of contact who will be ultimately in charge of recognizing, addressing, or resolving any issue that may have an impact on how people perceive your brand.

5. Representatives need training to understand how to react both proactively and reactively in a variety of situations, much like in customer service.
Don't only place the social media savvy individual in front of
the trademark.
6. Take on the qualities you want to communicate and impart. Follow a set of rules for behaviour.
7. Pay attention to the cultural norms of behaviour in each network and modify your outreach efforts appropriately.
8. Evaluate your grievances, pain areas, and levels of happiness in order to build deep relationships.
9. Take on the role of an actual participant in any community you want to engage in. Go beyond sales and marketing.
10. Avoid using pre-prepared remarks while addressing crowds. With every interaction, provide direction, value, and wisdom.
11. Give your delegates the authority to propose incentives and solutions.

12. Do more than simply listen and play along. Take action.

13. Ensure that all external operations are backed by an extensive infrastructure that can handle emergencies and adjust to changing market circumstances.
and requests.

14. Take lessons from every interaction and provide employees with a way to modify and enhance goods and services.

15. Create, provide, and uphold value and service consistently.

16. Establish relationships by working together and empowering advocacy.

17. Avoid being misinterpreted. Make sure your engagement aligns with goals established for the social media platform and that your message and aim are apparent.

18. For as long as it's crucial to your company, build and maintain positive connections both offline and online.

19. "Un-campaign" and develop continuing initiatives that help you stay involved on a daily basis.

20. "Un-market" by helping your community by volunteering your time.

21. Return the favour, show gratitude, and acknowledge noteworthy contributions from members of your respective communities.

Something to Keep in Mind:
Participation is the most crucial metric, particularly early on. A useful link is one that is actively maintained.

CHAPTER 5: MONITORING DATA & INSTRUMENTS

Measuring LinkedIn marketing performance and development is called tracking. LinkedIn has resources to assist you in doing this. A lot has been published on monitoring social media activities, calculating return on investment, and other subjects that have alarmed businesses worried about their reputation, privacy, and other issues.

Fortunately, LinkedIn offers a range of tools and statistics that make it quite simple.
Not to worry. When you initially start out, monitoring is easy: if you have more followers and a higher interaction rate, you are doing something well. If readers find your comments and information interesting

- If others decide to follow you
- If the majority of remarks are favourable

- If demands for individual assistance, counsel, judgments, or cooperative ventures increase

You're doing a good job! Eventually, you should keep track of:

1. Movement of Traffic
2. Interaction
3. Leads
4. Participation
5. Public perception of your brand or organization

As an aside, allow two to three months for your efforts to bear fruit. Before they will interact with you, others need to trust you. Avoid attempting to rush the procedure. Allow things to unfold organically.

We'll talk about several excellent tracking tools shortly, even if you have little money and are a horde of one.

Your company will flourish, expand, and develop when you pay attention to your consumers, regardless of whether they interact with you online or offline. Customers who are engaged are more responsive to your brand, convert faster, make purchases more often, and use word-of-mouth marketing to spread the word about you they become your own sales force!

These days, offering relevant material is one way to encourage consumer interaction. Take note that I didn't just say "content."The secret to connecting with your audience is relevance. Which sort of relevant material are you most likely to be able to provide? material that others in your neighbourhood want.

Keywords were the world's most essential thing a few years ago. However, there isn't much "community relevance" in keywords.
This is the reason why:

Usually, a company owner creates a website, posts his offerings, and uses relevant keywords to improve the site. The client uses Google (or another search engine), enters terms and phrases that are descriptive, and presto!
A selection of relevant web pages appears. The search engine has already completed the hard work of identifying which websites are relevant and presenting them to the user.

However, keyword-based search has been greatly altered by social media.
Owners of businesses need to do more than just put up a website and cross their fingers.
Social media platforms like Facebook, Twitter, LinkedIn, and others have moved the focus of search and its more important relative, engagement, from keywords to content relevance.

Nowadays, genuine interaction with the appropriate material at the appropriate moment is the only method to connect with your target audience. Robert Grant, the creator of Crowd

Conversion, says, "It's not a matter of if we're going to accept this. It is going to take us in. It is impossible to escape being impacted by these developments. [Will you] take advantage of this or will you just watch for others those who understand to enter and take over the area? We must begin interacting with clients right away. When you engage your consumer base meaningfully, you can:

1. Spend less money acquiring new clients.
2. Boost earnings
3. Cut expenses 4. Boost productivity

Keep in Mind: Word-of-mouth generated by engagement affects page rank. Cursed be the marketer who hasn't invested the effort to cultivate a rapport with his target audience.

CHAPTER 6: HANDLING REPUTATIONS

Reputation management may become essential if you learn how to effectively manage your online presence and as your following grows. Managing your online reputation allows you to regulate what the public knows about you or your business. Reputation management is rapidly gaining popularity because of the abundance of technologies available to search, consolidate, and distribute all kinds of information.

Good public relations is the aim of reputation monitoring. The creator of Reputation 24/7 in the United Kingdom, Nathan Baker, asserts that a person's or company's reputation is its most precious asset. Building a reputation takes time, a lot of work, and years of dedication. However, all it takes to destroy it is one disgruntled client, disgruntled worker, or nefarious rival."

Think of eBay as a customer review site. Based on consumer input, eBay enables ratings for both buyers and sellers. This assists others in making critical purchasing choices. Although we now take this system for granted, it was originally a novel idea.

Naturally, reputation involves more than just minimizing or eliminating unfavourable remarks or evaluations. Monitoring and managing one's reputation alsoincreases client satisfaction improves the impression of a brand acquires knowledge about rivals preserves the wealth of shareholders expands knowledge of the connection between conventional media and user-generated content. Early warning methods for defensive and reactive PR are provided.

lowers marketing expenses and aids in finding market gaps for goods and services improves understanding of user-generated content's keyword and keyphrase use and web networks

Point to Recall: You can guarantee that someone is talking about you online if you have a blog, landing page, e-commerce website, or several social media accounts. Remain alert and prepared to address bad situations promptly.

Elixir Systems has a great PDF on this subject. I strongly advise you to look into it further if it piques your interest. This paper suggests, among other things, creating a manual "early warning system" using Internet monitoring technologies to collect data and identify possible patterns. Among the recommended tools are:

Creating Google/Yahoo Alerts to track mentions of your brand in media Utilizing services like Technorati and Feedster to monitor blogs about your brand RSS reader customization for brand monitoring keeping track of important staff names, business, product, and brand names keeping an eye on sites relevant to the business

Additional information monitoring is advised by Elixir Systems, including "competitive brands and organizations, industry terms, as well as general industry news."

Not nearly prepared to handle your reputation? Just participate in the discussion. You play a major role as an influencer. The way you participate may influence others' perceptions. Take the lead in brand discussions and show people that your business is concerned about how the public perceives it.

CHAPTER 7: DEDICATION _LINKEDIN AN HOUR A DAY

I get asked this question a lot: "How do you find the time to be on LinkedIn so much? I find it difficult to even begin.
Usually, a variant of the query "Does LinkedIn really help you?" follows this. I ask you, did it bring you any actual business?

"Is all of this effort worth it?" is the thought that comes to mind. "Would I be chatting with you now if it weren't?" is how I respond to that.

A. IS ONE HOUR A DAY SUFFICIENT?

Are you competent where you work now? On the first day or first week, were you as skillful as you are now? You definitely got better with practice. Two popular justifications for not engaging in LinkedIn marketing are insufficient knowledge and lack of time.

It is easier to let go since there is so much information accessible (and often, the advice is contradictory) and our days are so full. It is simpler to persuade yourself that your company can function without LinkedIn. Another anxiety brought on by information overload is "Which method is right for me?" "How can I mess up?" "What happens if I look foolish?"

Good news. It's not all up to you to do! You'll have plenty of time to sell your goods and services on LinkedIn if you follow certain steps in precise ways and tune out the noise. Actually, you may reduce that hour to 20 to 30 minutes per day and still have excellent outcomes. Because I do it, I am aware.

Of course, if you really want to, you can do it all: create a ton of accounts, engage in pointless online chats, exhaust yourself while doing research, disregard technologies that may essentially simplify your life, and generally act

like a headless virtual chicken. There are
hundreds of social media platforms available.
Don't you hear about new ones every day? The
idea of community building has become quite
popular. We seem to be just now starting to
realize its true scope and potency.
To reap the rewards, however, you don't have to
be active everywhere. Anyone who asserts
otherwise is only giving false counsel. LinkedIn
is the ideal tool for achieving the kind of focused
thought that is necessary while concentrating on
lead creation.

Thus, inhale deeply first. Once you have
mastered the art, go crazy!
However, avoid setting yourself up for failure by
attempting to please everyone at once.
According to Reid Hoffman, one of LinkedIn's
co-founders, the platform's greatest use is the
chance to do "small goods" for other people.
Congratulate connections on their
accomplishments, provide a succinct response to
a query from the industry, or "like" an item that a
connection has posted.

The finest networking is advantageous to both parties. If you assist others, they will probably help you in return. The rest is like frosting on a cake.

If you follow Reid's recommendations. your presence and LinkedIn marketing outcomes will both grow on their own. Above all, keep your manners in mind.

On the other side of that display, there are people! Remain upbeat, kind, and real in your actions. Make invites and recommendation requests unique. Be kind while responding on online forums. LinkedIn is a valuable professional resource. As they say, "Don't do it anywhere you wouldn't say it or say it in public."

CHAPTER 8: SECTIONS OF A LINKEDIN PROFILE

Everyone in the advertising industry is aware of the enormous impact that a well-crafted commercial can have. Displaying your logo during the Super Bowl is insufficient; effective advertisements draw viewers in, emphasize the features of their products, and convey key brand messages.

It holds true for your LinkedIn profile as well. Although your profile is technically not advertising, it should still be a potent marketing tool that draws in your target market, highlights your unique selling proposition, and makes it clear to others how your solution can help them solve their problems.

If you attempted to make your LinkedIn profile "great" but gave up in frustration and it has been

inactive ever since, my bet is that you gave up.
Or maybe you lost motivation since you were
unable to see LinkedIn's true advantages.
Success on LinkedIn starts with a well-crafted
profile. You'll see articles comparing your
profile to a resume all over the Internet. False. It
goes much beyond that.

Without even making a phone contact, your
LinkedIn profile is a keyword-searchable
treasure that can place you in front of important
decision-makers. With a paper resume, try that!
Let's commit to treating your LinkedIn profile
with the decency it deserves.

The centerpiece of all of your LinkedIn
activities, the Profile is made up of many
sections. In the profile, you will discover:
headline
Status Reports
Synopsis of Suggestions
Experience
Expertise
Details of Contact

Links to presentations, your blog, etc.
Some people are unaware that LinkedIn page rank is somewhat dependent on keywords, much like Google. Using keywords facilitates people's ability to locate and engage with you, which should lead to more chances.
However, with millions of other users, how can you possibly compete?

A. THE "SECRET" OF LINKEDIN HEADLINE OPTIMIZATION

The space just after your name on the LinkedIn page is known as the Title or Headline, and it is the most crucial element to optimize. The majority of individuals indicate their work title here. However, just mentioning your work title might hinder you.

My title used to say something like "Results-Oriented Copywriter" a while back.

Not very fascinating, and it didn't help me
advance my knowledge of customer relationship
management and social media marketing.
I believed it to be effective. I was in error. This
is the reason why:
The 'people search' function on LinkedIn will
help more people discover you.
and establish a connection with you when your
title makes use of the appropriate keywords
since they are more likely to look up individuals
based on their work title than on your unusual
name (unless they are previously acquainted).
You are undoubtedly aware of the significance
of keywords for typical Internet searches.
However, most individuals are unaware that the
same guidelines apply to finding and acquiring
clients on LinkedIn.

For the purpose of crafting a compelling title tag,
there are many "recommended formulas." This is
the one that I like the best:
Trust/Credibility | Value or Solution | Value or
Solution | Who I Am

Instead of only describing yourself in terms of your job description, you may use this approach to explain what you do and how you help others solve challenges.

This is the headline I just wrote:

LinkedIn expert, LinkedIn coach for lead generation, LinkedIn speaker, author, and top 5 for "LinkedIn"

I started by considering what I do. Not simply the phrases that are usually connected to my business, but also the benefits I provide. Next, I thought about how I support other people and what attributes I wanted other people to see in me.

I then searched the LI network for keywords. How can you ever stand out if 367,589 other members also identify as "Marketing Director" and you name yourself that since it's part of your job description? With this term, your chances of appearing on LinkedIn's first page are zero.

And why is it important for us to be on page one? Because it's likely that the individual looking for a marketing director won't look at profiles beyond page two. If he or she is ambitious, maybe page 3.

As a result, quickly search for the terms you want to utilize using these keywords:

1) Open the LI screen's search box in the upper right corner.

2) Ensure that "People" is selected in the search box.

3) Enter the phrase in the box.

You'll get a list of all the people in your network who are using this word. Click on the little drop-down menus to switch the list's view to Expanded View and Keywords at the upper left of this list not your page.

This list has a number at the top right along with the word "results" (e.g., "7,019 results"). These are the rivals on LinkedIn.

You now know the number of people in your network who are using the same term or phrase. LinkedIn allows you to quickly examine how others have used the term and how they have ranked by utilizing it. If you have a premium account, LinkedIn neatly indicates where and how the phrase is used in each profile. The next step is to use the algorithm to determine how to define oneself in innovative terms that are simultaneously searchable, correctly descriptive, and not too competitive.

You have a total of just 120 characters at your disposal.

Can you see how, rather than just listing your occupation, a headline like this gives readers a quick overview of who you are, how you serve others, and the value you bring?

You would connect with more impact if all you did to enhance your profile was write a headline that grabbed attention.

B. SPECIALTIES

Here is a list of your most critical competencies, written in terms relevant to the sector. Your specialties will assist in drawing people to you when they search the LinkedIn database for someone with your kind of skill set.

A computer programmer with expertise in using
a complex software platform, for instance, might
wish to indicate this ability here.
Consider how other people could search. To
identify someone similar to you, use words and
phrases that most closely resemble the terms that
others could put in.

C. SUGGESTIONS

Although the recommendations area is
professionally validated, many LinkedIn users
are unaware of this:
For the sake of argument, your profile would
rank better if you had a clone and it had four
recommendations compared to yours, which had
five.

This little example highlights how crucial it is to
keep in mind that you are in competition with
other users on LinkedIn, especially when

recruiters use passive recruiting, which involves locating and getting in touch with users whose profiles fit job criteria even when those users aren't actively looking for work.

You also compete when a member requests expert assistance, requires certain skills to finish a job, or seeks an expert.

D. STATUS UPDATES

LinkedIn advises users with more than 500 connections to submit a status update three times a week. There are not 500 contacts on LinkedIn for the typical user. In light of this, how often should you update, and how much is too much? As a quick guideline, if individuals are complaining, requesting to be "removed from your list," or if the conversation has completely stopped, you are posting too often.

Make thoughtful decisions, ensure that your postings are relevant to your audience, elicit participation from others by asking questions,

and don't forget to reply to comments in order to maintain the flow of the discussion.
You'll know you're on the right road when comments and "likes" start to roll in.

E. THINGS TO POSTS

One often asks themselves, "What should I say?" Updates on the status should be instructive. It might be suitable to provide news about your business, brand, or industry. Nobody is very interested in hearing about your trip plans unless you're trying to make connections with other people who are going to the same event. Press releases, articles, stories from across the globe, and other generally intriguing links work well. Don't forget to stay current. Don't abruptly start posting chicken recipes if you are followed for your fantastic financial advice.

LinkedIn is a place to connect. It seems like a lot of individuals are hesitant to post their contact details online. However, the majority of professionals have a phone, email, and company address. This is not a secret; you can probably find it elsewhere on the Internet. If you work from home and are uncomfortable sharing your phone number, just provide your company email address.

Your worries about privacy and security are legitimate. I wouldn't disclose my birthday or marital status, for instance. Who gives a damn? However, A transaction may be made or broken by having easy access to a phone number, and it has.

Consider it. Proceed with what suits you best.

G. GROUPS

You have the option to create your own groups or join ones that are run by other LinkedIn users.

If you're not a seasoned LinkedIn user, you should probably join several existing groups to get a feel for the system first.

To see the groups:

Open your homepage.

Select the "Groups" tab.

Select "Groups Directory" using the drop-down menu.

Once there, you may use keywords to search for certain groups.

As of this writing, 1,025,115 groups are listed on LinkedIn. It makes sense why individuals are unsure of what to do and reluctant to take action! You may sign up for up to 50 groups. (A few groupings have smaller groups. These don't go toward the total for your group.)

Certain organizations welcome everyone as a member. Some demand that the group administrator or moderator personally accept your membership.

As previously said, you may want to go over your groups once a month or so to see which ones are still important and which ones can be eliminated or swapped out for ones that are more pertinent.

In groups, participation is crucial. It is your responsibility to log in, participate in conversations that have been posted, and initiate new ones. This is an excellent method to connect with people, demonstrate your skills, and bring value to the group.

Being able to communicate with other members without needing to know their email addresses is one of the finest features of group membership. You may ask for a connection only by sharing the same group.

On his website, CAREEREALISM, executive development specialist Andy Robinson provides insightful guidance on group building.

Important actions you may take in the Group

Post interesting online blog posts that you discover that group members might find interesting as "News Items" in the group forums. You may also share other helpful internet stuff, such as news, events, book recommendations, etc.

Posting links to YOUR own blog posts YOU
send letters to as many appropriate groups as
you can. I often cross-post my blog entries to
five to ten pertinent Groups, greatly expanding
the article's reach and maximizing the number of
individuals who may find the guidance and
knowledge inside the post helpful.
Engage in meaningful conversation in the group
forum. Make perceptive, upbeat remarks; enrich
discussions; provide counsel when needed; and
respond to inquiries.
Make use of the Groups "Jobs" function. Look
for employment or post-job vacancies. Groups
are a great place to find "niche" employment,
therefore anybody actively looking for work
should utilize them.

Get in touch with other Group members directly.
Look for individuals with whom you may
connect who have similar interests, experiences
working for a company, or going to school. On
LinkedIn, groups are a great way to grow your
direct connection network.

Form a group of your own! As the group activity moderator, establish your own "community." Your "brand" or area(s) of expertise are strengthened and you get excellent exposure when you moderate and exercise group "ownership." While looking for a group to join, take into account the following suggestions: Sector-specific Associations Retail industry groups, groups focused on health care, travel industry groups, etc. are a few examples. Groups of Trade and Professional Organizations Numerous professional and commercial associations have groups. Join those who are pertinent to you.

Employer Alumni Associations: There are alumni groups for several of the Fortune 100+ firms' previous workplaces. This is a fantastic method to get in touch with previous coworkers.

University/College Groups: The majority of prestigious institutions and schools have LinkedIn alumni organization groups. An additional fantastic method for getting in touch with "long lost" acquaintances and connections. Groups Related to Jobs and Careers. In the fields of employment, career development, and career management, there are hundreds of groups. You should absolutely check them out if you're looking for work.

Social Network Communities: Groups exist on LinkedIn, Facebook, and Twitter where users may discuss strategies, tactics, and other really helpful information pertaining to the majority of the main social networking platforms. Executive groups at the peer level. Examine the several categories dedicated to CEOs, COOs, CIOs, CFOs, etc. A terrific approach to share helpful knowledge and establish connections with experts at the same level.

Technical and Functional Specialty Groups: These come in scores upon scores. Locate a group or groups that are relevant to your functional or technical specializations (supply chain, IT, marketing, sales, and so on).

Interest groups of a personal kind. a passionate cyclist? There are, in fact, Groups. An avid supporter of a football team? Groups exist. An excellent means of sharing with others who have similar interests.

Fresh Enterprise: Look for groups to join where the members have a high probability of becoming your future clients, purchasers, influencers, and consumers. Seek methods to enrich these groups with conversation and information exchange.

Above all, avoid restricting your membership to organizations composed only of friends or colleagues. Join organizations where you may network and make new contacts to expand your social and professional horizons. For instance, while not being a RealtorTM, I am a member of a real estate association.

Since I'm the only one in the group discussing social media and LinkedIn, I've found new business in this group. Talk about setting oneself apart! However, I recently joined a sales organization whose members did not value Internet marketing, and I soon left. The majority of conversations focused on "old school" sales methods. I left as soon as I realized that this wasn't the group for me.

H. TOP INFLUENCER

An additional advantage is being designated as a Top Influencer, a title bestowed to a group member whose discussion subject garners a substantial amount of comments (i.e., group member involvement). Every week at the start, the Top Influencer "counter" resets to zero, providing every group member with an equal chance to succeed.

In order to encourage participants in group conversations rather than those who post often but don't engage, LinkedIn created Top Influencer.

Seeing your name on the list makes me very happy. It makes an impression on others. It demonstrates that you are thinking and participating since you are offering the appropriate questions. Additionally, recognizing the names of those who have been named Top Influencers is another chance for you to reach out and say "Congratulations!" All of these are good reasons to participate often.

I. "REPLIES AND ANSWERS"

"One of the best places to share business knowledge:" LinkedIn Answers, the part dedicated to general inquiries and answers Pose your query and get prompt, precise responses from your network and other professionals globally respond to inquiries to demonstrate your knowledge and skill.
Keep abreast with developments in your field and business.
Posing a Question

Access your home page by logging in.

Select the "More" tab.

Select "answers" using the drop-down menu.

Put your query in the space provided.

Choose the relevant category.

Choose whether you want to ask the question of certain links directly.

Asking Advice:

Your query will be answered right away under the Answers tab, on your profile, on the homepages of your connections, and—if you've chosen to have certain connections get it—in an email.

If you would rather ask a private question, you may do so and it will show up in the inboxes of people you have selected to get responses from, rather than on the internet.

Answers should not be used to advertise employment, hire candidates, etc. Questions of this kind will be marked and deleted.

Use the Advanced Answers search function to see whether someone has already asked and answered a question similar to yours.

Responding to an Inquiry

One of the best ways to demonstrate your expertise is to answer questions.

Do you recall my prior advice to monitor any upgrades to your network? Among the causes is this. On your homepage, you'll see questions posed by other members of your network, where you may readily contribute your knowledge. Additionally, you may use the Advanced Answers search or look up questions under the Answers tab.

You just need to click on the question to be sent to a page with all of the responses. When you answer, the person who posed the question will get an email as well as your response appearing on this page, your profile, and the home pages of your connections. You also have the option to respond to the inquiry in private.

Which of these websites would you want to utilize to promote your brand?
https://www.linkedin.com/profile/view?id=2471 9905&authType=name&authTo ken=6M2t&goback=%2Econ, or
https://www.linkedin.com/in/yourname
To further demonstrate your professionalism, change your profile settings to receive the public profile link, often known as the "vanity URL."
To generate a unique URL for you:
Access your profile by logging in.
Select "Edit Profile."
Select Public Profile Settings located on the page's right side.
At the top of the blue box, next to "Your Public Profile URL," click "edit."

After entering your last and first names in the box, choose "set address."
While you're here, you may also want to take the time to check your settings and the way others

see your profile. Make any adjustments that seem appropriate.

The HTML codes that you may use to make personalized buttons to advertise your profile on your blog, web pages, résumé, and other materials are also accessible on this page. Look it over. There are many options.

K. DIFFERENTIAL PROCEDURES FOR LINKEDIN INVITATIONS

Who on LinkedIn should you ask to join you? Individuals you are acquainted with Individuals you want to be acquainted with LinkedIn users not on LinkedIn. To finish the invitation, you'll need the recipient's email address unless you two are in the same group.
Try these suggestions:
1. Reach out to one person at a time:

On the profile page, under Contacts, click the "Add Connections" link and enter the person's name and email address.

2. Send a personalized message and invite each contact one at a time:

Click the "Add to your Network" link, which is bright yellow.

3. Select "people you may know" by clicking Contacts (a).

b) Select "Add Connectivity."

d) Select Potential Contacts.

As an alternative, click either a) Contacts or b) Add Connections.

c) To import your email addresses, click Continue in the blue box on the right-hand side just under your email address.

Alternatively: Type each person's email address into the blue box on the left-hand side to invite them.

4. Ask your coworkers or other students:

During the same time periods you have specified, colleagues have worked or are now working for one of the firms you have listed on your profile.

Companions have gone to the same schools that you have shown on your profile, during the times that you have indicated. Use the same procedures as above to connect with coworkers; however, choose Colleagues or Classmates rather than People You May Know and fill in the fields that appear on the page.

NOTE: You cannot include links or website URLs in an invitation sent via LinkedIn. Sharing of this data is restricted until the link is approved.

CHAPTER 9: COMPANY PAGES

Utilizing company pages as a research tool might help you identify and investigate businesses that you would want to work with. You may examine the business profile, the LinkedIn users who work there, and other forms of exclusive information on the corporate page. The LinkedIn blog included an article by Paul-Henri Ferrand, CMO of Dell Consumer, Small and Medium Business, about the then-new Dell corporate profile, to demonstrate the process.

Being a firm that conducts over 50% of its business online, Dell is aware that consumers' purchasing habits have fundamentally altered in this new age of e-commerce.

At Dell, we also see this move toward social commerce as a fantastic chance to keep fostering stronger bonds with our clients. Our Ratings &

Reviews site, which is hosted on Dell.com, our activity on Twitter, and the Business Solutions Exchange group on LinkedIn allows customers to easily share experiences and benefit from the knowledge of their peers. As a pioneer in the online space, we have been active in social commerce and support for a while.

We introduced the Business Solutions Exchange group on LinkedIn last summer in collaboration with Intel, enabling our clients to use their combined knowledge to inform purchasing choices. Our dedication to being active on the top social media platforms is reaffirmed on our newly created LinkedIn Company Page.

The updated LinkedIn company page for Dell We are pleased to report that, with the addition of a new product and service option to our LinkedIn Company Page, we have advanced the integration of online purchasing with social media. One of the several businesses making use of this new LinkedIn function, which enables users to post recommendations that are connected to their professional profiles, is Dell.

This new platform gives us a direct way to communicate and interact with all of our clients, big and small, while our past social commerce endeavors are mostly focused on consumers and small businesses.
Our recently launched Company Page offers our clients the chance to learn from us as well as from one another. At Dell, giving customers an amazing experience is essential.

Our clients rely on us to provide them with technological solutions that enable them to accomplish more at work, home, school, or anywhere else on the globe. In order to do this, Dell successfully communicates with over 5.4 million consumers each day via phone, in-person, on Dell.com, and, more and more, social media platforms like LinkedIn.
With more than 60,000 followers on my LinkedIn company page, I'm interested in

observing which goods and services generate the most online discussion.

A. LOCATING BUSINESS PROFILES

Click the "Companies" tab located in the top navigation bar to be taken to the Company Search page. Also, you can find out which businesses are the most linked, fastest-growing, and most seen here.

As an alternative, each member profile associated with a firm has a unique symbol next to the name of that company. The emblem resembles a sheet of paper that has been folded down on the right side. To read the business profile, click the company name or just move your cursor over the symbol to bring up the company page. The following advice comes from LinkedIn:

Elements of a Business Profile

After a short summary, corporate profiles include two main sections: data on relevant individuals within the organization on the left and compiled employee statistics on the right.

Associated Businesses

Have you ever wondered where former workers of a firm went or where they worked before leaving? or which other businesses they have the strongest ties to?

Related Companies look for patterns in people's work histories and establish links between different businesses.

Important Data

Have you ever wondered which areas or which schools a firm prefers to employ from? The aggregated non-personally identifiable data of LinkedIn members who are presently employed by this firm is used to create Key Statistics.

This information is not supplied or supported by the firm; it merely represents estimations of its workforce.

Company Description: Our partner Capital IQ has supplied a brief synopsis of the company.

Workers of the Company

a list of people in your network on LinkedIn who are now employed by this organization, separated by no more than three degrees.
Fresh Appointments LinkedIn users whose bios show they just joined this organization.
Current Changes and Promotions
users of LinkedIn whose profiles show they just changed jobs at this organization.

Well-liked Profiles

These are LinkedIn individuals who are featured because they are regularly the outcome of searches and other actions conducted inside the LinkedIn network, mentioned in blogs, involved in industry organizations, and/or engaged in the press. Individuals on this list have some of the highest prominent opinions inside their organization.

How Data Is Collected

Capital IQ and LinkedIn user data are the two sources of information that you see on corporate sites. The fundamental business information, including revenue and company overview, was supplied by our partner Capital IQ. The aggregated corporate statistics and all pertinent individuals are derived from LinkedIn network data. (End of item cited on LinkedIn)

B. MAKING A PROFESSIONAL REPORT

Access your home page by logging in.
Select the More tab.
Select Companies using the drop-down menu.
Select "Add a Company" from the menu on the right.
Observe the instructions.
Recall that before you can build a new firm page, your profile has to include this firm as a previous or current employer.

The "Improve Your Profile" button, located on the right side of your profile page, is a new feature for LinkedIn profiles. When you click this button, you'll get some quick ideas on what you might add to your profile to make it better.

D. GETTING THE INFORMATION YOU REQUIRE

A lot of new, relevant information is required for social media marketing. Where is it located? Consider basing your content search on these well-liked items:

top news items, particularly those pertaining to a certain industry

Social Networks Methods

Things pertaining to web traffic, such as page rank, trends, and strategy

views of well-known individuals (such as industry professionals)

Every kind of information and data

It seems that everyone enjoys these snippets
from Google News.
Lists (like "7 Most Wanted" or "Top 10 Ways
to...")
Future events your network may find interesting

www.ingramcontent.com/pod-product-compliance
Lightning Source LLC
Chambersburg PA
CBHW050042260726
48658CB00005B/1722